HOW TO LEAD A CHILD TO CHRIST

HOW TO LEAD A CHILD TO CHRIST

Daniel H. Smith

MOODY PRESS

CHICAGO

© 1987 by
DANIEL H. SMITH

All Scripture quotations, unless noted otherwise, are from the *New American Standard Bible*, © 1960, 1962, 1963, 1968, 1971, 1973, 1975, and 1977 by The Lockman Foundation.

The author is indebted to Lewis E. Raths, "Emotional Needs and Teacher Training," *Journal of Educational Sociology* 24, no. 7 (March 1951): 369-432, for his list of eight basic psychological needs of children.

Library of Congress Cataloging in Publication Data

Smith, Daniel H., 1933-
    How to lead a child to Christ.

    1. Children—Conversion to Christianity.
2. Children—Religious life. I. Title.
BV4925.S48   1987   259'.22   86-23913
ISBN 0-8024-4622-1

2 3 4 5 6 7 Printing/VP/Year 91 90 89 88 87

Printed in the United States of America

To my children

Contents

Contents

Introduction

The night seemed unusually dark even thirty feet from the blazing camp fire. Only an occasional mosquito interrupted my thoughts as I prepared for camp testimonies. Campers came in groups, each with a counselor. The program director led the group in singing, defined a testimony, and asked for volunteers.

The first nervous camper spoke so quietly I could not hear. I blamed it on my age. Then I realized that all of the campers around me also missed the testimony.

The second camper detailed his first camp experience several years before. He abruptly concluded by saying, "And on the last night of camp I wanted to be saved, and I went and talked to my counselor, and he saved me."

Before I had time to assess his statement, another camper described how he had been sitting at a camp fire several years before, and while looking into the burning fire became fearful of going to hell. He concluded by saying, "So I went and talked to my counselor, and we got down on our knees, and I got saved."

The fourth camper didn't actually give a testimony. He picked up on the theme of hell and preached to the unsaved campers, reminding them that the camp fire was cool compared to the flames of hell. Soon another camper told about dreaming that he was in hell after seeing a movie about a burning house. He said he woke up crying and was aware of his mother's presence. He said his mother told him he must have got saved through the experience. He sat down.

I do not remember the three or four testimonies that followed. My mind was wildly racing. I was disturbed at what I heard. Not one camper mentioned Christ; in fact, there was little doctrine and a great deal of individuals picking up on certain cues from the previous speaker. If I had been unsaved, there was no way those statements would have helped me understand the need for salvation.

Over the years that kind of experience has been repeated many times. In fact, I characteristically come away from children's testimonies very troubled. On many occasions I have talked with children who have given their testimonies and have found that many do not have a clear definition of salvation.

Now let me illustrate my concern for the other side. I once directed a children's camp in which most of the staff was recruited by others. Camp started on a Sunday. Monday evening one of the staff members reported that she had led twenty-one children to the Lord that day. It dawned on me that she had spoken to me on Sunday evening as well, also reporting a number of children that she had "led to the Lord." I recognized a pattern. Each evening during that week she reported to me how many kids she led to the Lord. I kept a total beginning with Monday night. By Friday night her total exceeded the number of campers, and we still had one more day to go!

During that week many staff members became displeased with that woman, who would interrupt children's conversations and interrogate them with leading questions that inevitably led campers to answer yes to the question, "Do you want to be a Christian?"

My experiences may seem either realistic or extreme, depending on your perspective. But they do illustrate the issues that have concerned me about how others lead children to Christ.

Perhaps at no time in church history has there been more emphasis upon children's ministries. Sunday school has continued into its third century, and a proliferation of children's ministries including Bible camps, clubs, and other innovative programs have been developed as well.

Many adults specialize in children's ministries. This group includes a large number of skilled individuals who prepare curriculum and plan programs as well as those who minister as staff and administer at various levels.

Progressive and growing churches will include specialized children's ministries. Many individuals who serve Christ begin in a children's ministry. Unfortunately, most have had no training or preparation. They either duplicate the methods of their teachers or launch out creatively.

Many argue that it is natural to work with children and specific training is not needed. This view also assumes that parenting is natural and does not require any training. One look at the vast array of books written about the breakdown of the family, however, would cause us to question the "no training needed" assumption.

But even in all the training available, whether in Christian liberal arts colleges, Bible colleges, or other specialized training programs, little prepares individuals to lead a child to Christ. Yet, in a sense, producing, publishing, and distributing curriculum materials and administering, teaching, or counseling all come to fruition when a child expresses his or her interest in being saved.

Many who work with children are either afraid of or perplexed by their task. Eternity may focus upon one young life and a few minutes of time. One may fulfill this task biblically and intelligently, avoid the situation, or do a faltering, shoddy job.

This brief study is a result of years of experience in working with children as well as concern about how others evangelize boys and girls.

I want to express appreciation for the many Christians who do a wise, sensitive, and spiritually intelligent job ministering to children. I have learned much from their ministries. My insights and suggestions are gleaned from a number of sources and a lot of experience. This study is presented with a prayerful desire that we all prepare ourselves to do a careful, credible, and biblical job in leading a child to Christ.

1

Biblical Foundations

Doctrine must provide the foundation for all of our service for Christ. That is specifically true when a ministry involves both Bible teaching and the delicate, sensitive touching of lives. There will be no attempt to exhaust doctrine here but rather to introduce areas of further personal study for those serious about leading children to the Savior.

THE BIBLICAL FOUNDATION

Any who desire a ministry with children should be careful to establish convictions from Scripture. First, we must establish the need for children to be saved. In essence that means we must recognize that children are sinners and need salvation.

1. *All children are born with a sin nature.* John 3:6-7 says, "That which is born of the flesh is flesh, and that which is born of the Spirit is spirit. Do not marvel that I said to you, 'You must be born again.' " David acknowledged that fact when he wrote, "Behold, I was brought forth in iniquity, and in sin my mother conceived me" (Psalm 51:5). Sin nature is transmitted from one generation to another. Scripture teaches that Adam's sin was imputed to all individuals (Romans 5:12).

2. *Early voluntary actions reflect a sinful nature.* You do not have to teach a child to rage, be selfish, deceive and lie, or be stubborn. An apple tree bears apples because it is by nature an apple tree. The bearing of apples in the fourth or fifth year is tangible evidence of the nature of the

tree. The psalmist observed that fact when he said that the wicked go astray from birth (Psalm 58:3).

It is difficult for those who live in a humanistic society to acknowledge these facts. Yet the Bible clearly testifies to them, and no generation has more completely verified the truth of these biblical statements than ours. Failing to recognize the true need of children will certainly lead to problems in our ministry with them.

3. *Children are in danger of a lost eternity.* Establishing the above matters doctrinally is necessary for all who take Scripture at face value. Consider the Lord Jesus' message in Matthew 18. In verse 11 He uses the word *lost,* and in verse 12 He uses the word *straying.* Later we will consider other teachings from this text, but at this point note that the Lord Jesus recognized that children were lost and in danger of eternal judgment. Our ministry to children will not be its best if we ignore or deny this fact.

4. *Scripture views children as sensitive to biblical truth, yet in danger of hardening.* Ecclesiastes 12:1 warns against the hardening of age and appeals to the reader to consider the Person and truth of the Creator at an early age.

5. *Children can be saved.* Scripture indicates that salvation is a matter of a responding to the gospel in childlike faith. The Lord teaches in Matthew 18:3: "Truly I say to you, unless you are converted and become like children, you shall not enter the kingdom of heaven." The mature faith of the theologian does not save; it is genuine childlike faith that brings salvation. A child does not need to become an adult to be saved; rather an adult needs to come in childlike faith to be saved.

6. *The Lord Jesus specifically invites children to come to Him.* Matthew 19:14 says, "Let the children alone, and do not hinder them from coming to Me." He saw the children's need, realized He could meet their need, and invited them to Himself for eternal salvation.

SAVED THE SAME WAY AS ADULTS

The fact that children are saved the same way adults are saved should be evident to any who have studied Scripture. The Bible presents only one way of salvation: "For by grace you have been saved through faith" (Ephesians 2:8). It is not uncommon, however, to find Sunday school material that teaches preschool children to "love Jesus."

The same material for primary age children tells them that they must trust in Christ for salvation. The implication is that although it is enough for little children to love Jesus, at a later point they must trust Him as Savior. This is doctrinally misleading. Children are saved the same way as adults. No one is saved by loving Jesus, and such material does not adequately present the gospel.

Some argue that young children are not able to understand the issues of faith and grace. I realize that children mature at different rates, and the ability to discern spiritual issues comes at a different point for different individuals. However, many have understood salvation by grace through faith at a very early age. We should present a consistent gospel message even to young children.

SAVED TO THE SAME DEGREE AS ADULTS

The Bible does not distinguish two different classes or categories of believers. The Bible also does not present stages or degrees of salvation. Receiving Christ as Savior results in salvation in its fullest sense. It is both complete and eternal. It is interesting to note that sometimes those who are most eager to present the gospel to children are the most suspicious when a child professes salvation. We make children wait years before we lead them on in the next steps of Christian growth, including baptism and church fellowship. This is a tacit denial of the genuineness of the salvation of the individual and lacks scriptural authority.

The concern of this book is to teach thoroughness and biblical accuracy in leading children to Christ. No doubt many boys and girls are unwisely urged into a false profession. But spiritually minded adults who know the Word of God and love children can discern genuine confessions by careful communication with children. There is no more biblical basis for doubting the genuine, intelligent, and uncoerced confession of faith from a child than there is from an adult.

UNDERSTANDING THE GOSPEL CLEARLY

"Salvation is from the Lord" (Jonah 2:9).

It takes a thorough understanding of the gospel and biblical terms to present the message at a child's level. We may unintentionally hide behind misunderstood terminology.

We must be able to present the great truths of the gospel, including redemption, reconciliation, and propitiation—terms that present the finished work of Christ—at the child's level. We must also be prepared to convey the glorious realities of justification, forgiveness, regeneration, and sanctification. If adults do not understand the doctrines of salvation sufficiently to present them so children can understand, then their tendency is either to use poorly chosen terminology or to burden the child with terminology that they themselves do not adequately understand. It is generally thought that just about anybody can work with children. However, to do an excellent job with boys and girls we may need an even more thorough knowledge of Scripture than would be needed in some ministries with young people or adults.

TERMINOLOGY

In light of the above discussion, we need to be careful with our terminology. Biblical terms such as *believe* and *faith* should be clearly understood, and the adult must be able to define and to describe these concepts. We should be flexible with our terminology and able to use other biblical terms such as *trust* and *receive*. Lacking the flexibility that comes from a thorough knowledge of Scripture and biblical terms makes us prone to resort to other terminology that is not biblical and often questionable, such as "accept Christ" or "let Jesus come into your heart."

NECESSITIES

A careful study of the New Testament yields basic ingredients that ought to be included in an adequate presentation of the gospel. Many who have written on the subject of personal evangelism have grappled with summarizing the gospel and reducing it to its most basic and necessary elements. This is particularly necessary in child evangelism because adding ingredients that are not essential biblical truths for salvation could unnecessarily complicate and delay the response of children to the gospel.

I realize that it may seem presumptuous for anyone to authoritatively conclude which elements of biblical truth constitute the total and essential elements of the gospel. But I suggest that the message certainly include the following:

1. *The nature of sin and the need of the individual.* In every gospel passage the need of the sinner is fundamental. The apostle Paul in Romans insists that "the wrath of God is revealed from heaven against all ungodliness and unrighteousness of men" (1:18). Although adults could unnecessarily frighten and disturb children by an undue emphasis upon this biblical truth, proper gospel presentation includes the need of the sinner and the fact of eternal judgment. What other reason would make one seek salvation?

Many point out that in a desire to avoid offense, some stumble into the pitfall of "easy believism." Many of the shallow and questionable conversions that now plague the church may well be the result of an inadequate presentation of man's lost condition. You do not need to shake children fearfully over the flames of hell. But the gospel message is not complete without a clear statement of the fact and nature of sin and the need of the individual for salvation through Christ.

2. *The Person and work of Christ.* All believers agree that the gospel necessarily has at its heart the Person of our Lord Jesus. In fact, He *is* our salvation. Salvation is not so much a state or an act as it is a Person. That is why John could say, "He who has the Son has the life" (1 John 5:12). If we are to be biblically correct, we must present Christ as the central Person and theme of the good news. Some understanding of both who He is and what He did in His death and resurrection are necessary in the gospel presentation. There is no finer preparation for evangelism than a thorough study of the Person and work of Christ.

3. *God's requirement for salvation.* God has taken the initiative in extending salvation and has given us the condition on which His salvation is offered and received. In essence that means that grace is God's part and faith is man's part. Neither of these realities should be complicated, diminished, or added to. To add to either grace or faith is to destroy their essential nature (Galatians 1:6-7). Any thought of salvation by human merit is strongly condemned in Scripture. An addition of a system of works—even in part—destroys the true nature of the gospel. God stated one condition for humans to meet: faith that finds its object in Jesus Christ. Any adequate presentation of the gospel includes a clear understanding of that one condition.

4. *Results.* Any adequate presentation of the gospel should include the biblical promise of that which God will give freely to the believer.

Children should have an answer to the question, "If I receive Christ as Savior, what will be the result in my life?" The ingredients of salvation, including forgiveness and cleansing, a right standing with God, placement in the family of God, and assurance of heaven should be included in the message.

The glorious dimensions of salvation are beyond comprehension. Even in eternity, we will learn more and more about all that God has provided for those who love Him and belong to Him. Yet it is unthinkable that we would present the salvation message to children without stating some of the results of trusting Christ.

Children sometimes believe that they will immediately become adults after receiving Christ. Others expect that they will suddenly become "A" students or never have any trouble getting along with their sisters, brothers, or friends. One of the best ways to avoid wrong expectations is to teach what Scripture teaches about faith in Christ.

CAUTION

Before we leave the issue of doctrinal matters, a word of caution: the adult's role can be wrongly seen, and the place of the evangelist overemphasized. Humans are instruments through which God works in presenting His truth. This is both a privilege and a responsibility of believers, and we rejoice in the fact that God uses humans to accomplish His work. Presumably He could send angels to do a more consistent and eloquent job of presenting the message. But it is to redeemed humans that He commits the ministry of reconciliation.

God reminds us, however, that although one human may plant the seed and another water the seed, it is God who gives the increase (1 Corinthians 3:7-9). From beginning to end, salvation is of the Lord.

We must honestly face Jesus' warning in Matthew 18: causing a little one to stumble is a serious offense (v. 6). No thinking Christian would want to come under the Lord's condemnation for doing a shoddy or careless job. Pushing a child into a false profession or failing to meet the opportunities to minister to a child can be considered as acts of stumbling.

2

Basic Needs of Children

Although doctrine is paramount in Christian service, human behavior must also be considered in any wise approach. Personalities are complex, and Scripture affirms that we are fearfully and wonderfully made (Psalm 139:14). There are, however, valuable lessons that we may learn from those who have studied human behavior. That is particularly true in the crucial matter of leading a child to Christ, for it is inevitable that a certain amount of emotional agitation will be present along with the spiritual battles that rage in the one facing Christ's claims.

BASIC PSYCHOLOGICAL NEEDS

Lewis Raths, a leading educator, defines eight basic psychological needs in all children. This summary is a helpful guideline for those who work with boys and girls.

BELONGING

Children have a need to belong to a group or individual that they consider significant. In fact, this need tends to increase throughout childhood until, in the teenage years, the need to belong seems almost desperate, sometimes dominating all else.

As we present the gospel, there is a sense in which we appeal to the need of the child to belong. One of the great Scripture promises is that upon receiving Christ as Savior, we are made members of the family of God (Galatians 3:26). We belong to Christ in the true sense of the word. That is a valid and positive appeal to children's needs. However, it is possible to wrongly appeal to this need and confuse the gospel. For example, if we create the atmosphere of "let's all go up and get saved," we may see some children following the crowd out of a sense of need to belong rather than true spiritual readiness.

ACHIEVEMENT

Children need to achieve, to feel that they are accomplishing something important. We may properly appeal to this need as we present the gospel. Commending children for understanding spiritual truths, as the Lord did with Peter (Matthew 16:17), or encouraging children to continue memorizing Scripture is certainly fitting. However, since the only thing an individual can do to "work the works of God" is to believe in Christ (John 6:28-29), care must be taken not to imply saving merit in human efforts. This includes actions such as coming forward, raising a hand, getting down on one's knees, talking to the speaker, or a number of other things that can be classified as human works.

FREEDOM FROM FEAR

Both Scripture (1 John 4:18) as well as personal experience teach us that fear is a powerful and uncomfortable emotion. The Bible teaches that it is a fearful thing to fall into the hands of the living God in unbelief and that God is a consuming fire (Hebrews 12:29). There is a reasonable and inevitable element of fear in response to the gospel. In fact, some who have come to Christ in later years have expressed the need for the terrifying and convicting work of the Spirit to bring them to their knees and their senses. However, it may be more harmful than helpful to overdo the element of fear when ministering to children. One concern that I have has arisen from listening to children give testimonies. It is worth noting that for many the major motivating factor was fear. Fear brings professions, but fear may be overdone in children's ministries.

Perhaps one reason so many children go into a period of spiritual stagnation in their teens is that they were frightened into "jumping on a fire escape" rather than being warmly attracted to the Person of Christ. Although the danger of a lost eternity is a part of the gospel, it is not the central issue. The central issue is the Person of Christ, and He attracts children to Himself today just as He did when he walked on this earth. I would strongly recommend that adults carefully monitor their tendency to overuse fear as a motivation, clouding true conviction with human emotion.

LOVE AND AFFECTION

Any who have worked with boys and girls know that they need love and affection. Some children show that need for love and affection more than others. Some children who have the need but don't know how to express it may seem distant. However, one can be sure that the need is universal, and this need may be properly appealed to in a gospel presentation. It would be sad if we failed to present a message that finds its origin in God's great love. Many have come to Christ primarily because of the message of John 3:16: "For God so loved the world. . ." And the message does not stop at that point. Scripture personalizes the message of a loving God in passages such as Galatians 2:20: "The Son of God. . .loved me, and gave himself for me" (KJV*). The gospel is a message of love, and we have the privilege of attracting children to a Savior who loves us and gave Himself for us.

Perhaps the most common abuse of this need has to do with the conduct of those who work with children. Adults may unwisely barter for children's love and use their own love for children as a leverage. Particularly in the case of children who are starved for love and affection, loving adults can easily get children to do things just to please them and to continue to experience their love. The "do this to please me" approach to the evangelism of children is hazardous. It may pre-empt the convicting work of the Spirit and lead to false professions, neurotic dependency, and eventual disillusionment.

In summary, the need for love and affection in some children may be so strong that they are vulnerable to adults' dynamics and gimmicks. May God give us genuine love for children. But may He also grant the

*King James Version.

spiritual sense to specialize in a presentation of His love and His saving grace and not merely to manipulate children.

FREEDOM FROM GUILT

Guilt, like fear, can be a powerful negative motivator. Unfortunately for some children, guilt becomes an effective tool that adults can use to control and manipulate. In a proper presentation of the gospel, there is a natural and healthy sense of guilt. The individual must sense the need for a Savior through an awareness of sin and guilt in the presence of God. When induced by right understanding of Scripture and the working of the Spirit, guilt is a positive motivating force.

However, as in the case of fear, guilt may be overworked in child evangelism. Adults can become masters at manipulating children through humanly imposed guilt and confuse or pre-empt the work of the Spirit. This is particularly a problem when mixed with the ability that some have to manipulate children into pleasing them personally through the use of guilt.

A proper presentation of the gospel includes the prospect of being cleansed from sin and guilt through the blood of Jesus Christ. May we faithfully present this message and not confuse the issue with any human manipulation or exaggerated psychological guilt.

CONTRIBUTING

Even though it may seem difficult to identify children's need for contributing since some have become discouraged and appear to lack this need, all children do need to feel that they are contributing something positive, something that is worthwhile to the situation and to others around them.

The existential philosophies of our Western world give children the compulsive need to contribute that we so vividly see in our young and middle-aged adults. In fact, this existential need to contribute may drive us into situations that are to our own detriment and cause us to miss the value of silence. We too soon learn to "let it all hang out." We ignore the biblical injunction "Let everyone be quick to hear, slow to speak and slow to anger" (James 1:19). We need to avoid the wrong impressions so commonly given to children that "if you're speaking your mind, you're great." Biblically speaking, greatness comes in controlling the tongue—in words that are fitly and aptly spoken—not in the pouring out of personal opinion and the public parading of things that are private or even sinful.

There is an appropriate sense in which we can encourage children to fulfill their need to contribute to the welfare of the group by planning activities that include participation. Children love to help. We may—in our laziness—overdo this by making a "go-fer" out of them. But we can positively use their energies and participation and discover their thoughts and emotions. A purely "sit and listen" context is difficult for children. Activity and personal participation can cultivate a receptive climate.

UNDERSTANDING AND KNOWLEDGE

It is refreshing to see children's inquiring minds expressed in their questions and childlike inquisitiveness. But it is alarming to see how quickly parents and teachers can squelch this by being too busy or too defensive to answer questions. In fact, sometimes adults are so successful in squelching inquiring children that by the time they get into the later grades, teachers long to have enough mental activity to result in genuine and meaningful questions.

The need to understand and know is inherent, and although it may vary from one individual to another, we can rest in the fact that God built this need into human beings (Proverbs 18:15). Let's show a proper respect for the mind with an honest presentation of biblical truth so that the Spirit of God may do His perfect work.

ECONOMIC SECURITY

A number of adults became concerned with the atmosphere prevailing in a certain Christian day school. The emphasis was on wearing just the right kind of clothes—expensive clothes—and doing the right kinds of costly things. Conversation with several students made apparent that this dominated the climate of the school. Those students whose parents were not affluent lived in fear and struggled with the prospect of being socially ostracized. The adults did well to be alarmed, for fear relating to economic security can completely overshadow any positive spiritual accomplishments through school programs.

It is conceivable that this same thing may inadvertently creep into our methodology in child evangelism. Great care must be taken on any occasions in which we take offerings or establish the pattern of dress or program activities. We may be in danger of violating the warning in James 2:1-4 at the child's level and missing the blessing of God in our ministries. In their need for economic security, children are supersensitive to competition for the materialistic ingredients of life. May we learn to share our Lord's compassion for the poor and the fatherless.

At this point let us summarize some conclusions that may be drawn from the recognized needs of all children. These are generalizations that are drawn from conversations with spiritually minded people who know children well and who have years of experience. There will be exceptions, but exceptions tend to accentuate the rule. These summary facts are:

1. *Children are more easily reached than adults.* Busy schedules along with hardening and self-centeredness make many adults virtually unreachable. If you sit on a park bench you will find few adults willing to stop and talk. However, sitting on the same bench you may find children responsive to a smile and friendly conversation. This vulnerability of children gives understandable concern to parents. But in the normal neighborhood children are far more easily reached with personal communication than are adults.

2. *Children are more easily taught than adults.* The relatively uncluttered and unbiased minds of children are receptive to biblical truth presented appropriately. Children have fewer erroneous ideas about religion than do adults. Characteristically, children can memorize Scripture at an astounding rate because of little interference with heavy responsibilities and conflicting patterns of thought. Even profound doctrine can be readily understood by children if presented skillfully.

3. *Children are more easily convicted than adults.* The process of growing older is frequently a process of spiritual hardening. The appeal to consider the things of God in one's youth is based upon this fact (Ecclesiastes 12:1).

4. *Children respond more easily to a gospel presentation.* Children have less social and personal restraint. The typical adult reaction —"What will others think?"—is not as pronounced in childhood. The sincerity and idealism of youth should be a tremendous encouragement in a ministry to them. As noted previously, adults unfortunately may take advantage of this idealism with various gimmicks that confuse the true issue. However, it is statistically obvious that most people who trust Christ do so in their youth.

5. *When a child trusts Christ, not only is a soul saved but a life is potentially saved.* A well-known preacher returned home after a Sunday night service to report to his wife that two-and-a-half people had been saved. His wife thought this was a way of saying that two adults and a child had been saved, but the spiritually wise preacher immediately clarified his intent by saying that two children and an adult had been saved. Although it is not always true that those who make a profession in childhood live a life for God, the potential of a life lived for God's glory should motivate us in our ministry to children.

In his old age, David commanded his soul to rise up and bless God for a number of benefits that he had known at the hand of God (Psalm 103). One of those benefits was that God had redeemed his life from destruction (v. 4). One idea inherent in the word *destruction* is the idea of wasting or squandering. In his youth David knew the joys of a relationship with God and often communed with Him and enjoyed His fellowship. Although his life was not without human frailty, David blessed God for sparing him from wasting his life. We may know individuals who came to Christ in their old age and regretted that they had not responded to the gospel earlier.

6. *Children who trust Christ ought to be led in the normal steps of Christian growth.* It is easy to rejoice in children's responses to the gospel and then let them languish for years before we become concerned about encouraging them into the normal steps of Christian growth.

Assurance of salvation, obedience of believer's baptism, instruction in personal growth, Bible study, and fellowship with other Christians are all necessary steps in Christian growth. Many believe that the reason those who profess salvation in childhood so often go into a period of spiritual doldrums in their teens is that they have not been led along in the normal pattern of growth and progress in spiritual things.

7. *"Remember that neither the Lord nor the apostle Paul went into children's work."* I remember the first time I heard that statement. As a Christian education teacher at a Bible school, I was stunned when an older, wiser colleague expressed this solemn truth. But after great consideration and discussion, the timely point was substantiated: children's work cannot stand alone. Old as well as young must be reached. The church is made up of all ages. In fact, a local church will never be built on children's ministries alone. We must keep children's ministries in perspective.

REPEATED PROFESSION

During a staff meeting at Bible camp, a counselor joyously reported that a camper had expressed an interest in salvation the previous night. He had talked with the boy, and he professed to be saved. Although other counselors were overjoyed, one was visibly disturbed. With consternation he reported that he had had this same boy in his cabin the previous year, and the boy had made a profession at that time. The whole group was perplexed and discussed at length why the repeated profession occurred.

This is not an uncommon experience in working with children. In fact, it appears that there are a number of reasons that children make repeated professions. This discussion is not exhaustive, but let us consider some of the factors that may be involved.

First, there may be the desire to repeat a pleasant experience. Believers delight to recall the sense of forgiveness and the joy of knowing that all is right between them and God in those happy moments after they received Christ as Savior. Added to that may have been the obvious joy—if not ecstasy—of individuals around them as they heard their first faltering confession of Christ. For many individuals that inner joy and ecstatic atmosphere is an extremely pleasant experience that would be enjoyable to repeat. Children are not schooled in the great doctrines of the faith and may not be conscious of the once-for-all work of God in salvation. Those who understand childish ways of thinking can readily recognize how some would be inclined to make another profession in order to repeat such a pleasant experience.

A second reason children make repeated professions is simply to please the person who is dealing with them. It is characteristic of children to want to please adults. Some adults who are particularly warm and outgoing can easily win an eager and naive response from them. After all, as we minister to a group of children we frequently encourage them as a group to be sure they have trusted Christ as Savior. We may tell them how urgently we want them to be saved, and while we are thinking of the unsaved individuals in the group, loving children who have already made a profession of salvation are hearing the same appeal. As you express your desire for them to get saved they may readily respond to please you.

A third reason children repeat their profession is that the previous profession may have *only* been a profession, and they are not truly saved. As we will note in a later discussion, it is easy to push or lead a child into making a mere profession without full understanding and without the maturity of conviction born of the Spirit of God. If the previous experience was only a profession and the sense of need and guilt continue, it may well be that the child genuinely needs to receive Christ.

A fourth reason children make repeated professions has to do with the lack of assurance of salvation. Some children do genuinely receive Christ but are never given a biblical foundation to have assurance of salvation. As a result, they live with doubts and fears and sustain a measure of guilt that is much like the conviction of the Spirit. Upon hearing the gospel and the urgency of salvation again, the uncertainty of assurance and residual guilt motivates them to make a profession of salvation again "just to be sure." Perhaps you can recall many individuals who have given testimony to the fact that they have struggled with doubt and lack of assurance over long periods of time and have made countless numbers of professions of salvation as a symptom of their lack of assurance.

The fifth possible reason children repeat professions has to do with the reality of sin. One of the wonderful dimensions of salvation is the presence of the Spirit. One of His ministries is to make us aware of sin that we commit as believers and the necessity of confessing and forsaking that sin. If children are not taught the fact of and the way to deal with sin, the sense of guilt and doubt that arises over unresolved sin in their lives may lead children to assume that they are not saved. That makes them vulnerable to repeated professions in an attempt to deal with guilt.

It seems apparent at this point that, with such a variety of reasons for children's repeating professions, adults must take sufficient time to deal with children and discern where the children really are spiritually. In some of these situations pushing children to make another profession may compound their spiritual difficulties rather than resolve them.

We must always deal with the problem of ego in our own conduct and ministry. We all want to be seen as individuals who have the privilege of leading children to Christ. In our eagerness to add another success case to our own record, we may convince a doubting child that he or she is not saved. We may find it difficult to be honest enough with ourselves and others to admit this tendency, but we all have this propensity in our eagerness to be successful. This kind of self-seeking should be confessed and forsaken as sin if we are to be truly useful instruments of God.

ATMOSPHERE

The relatively naive and impressionable nature of a child and the warning of our Lord Jesus to avoid causing offense to, or stumbling, a little child (Matthew 18:6) should motivate us to evaluate our methodology carefully. Sometimes intentionally and sometimes unintentionally we build into a situation factors that encourage responses not necessarily born of the Spirit. To push a child into a false profession is one way of causing a child to stumble. Think through the appeals made here and learn to evaluate your own methodology and the atmosphere that is created ministering to children.

A work of integrity will be intentionally free from gimmicks or tangible material rewards for professing faith in Christ. I can recall occasions when children who professed Christ were given candy bars. Even goldfish and puppies have been used as rewards to motivate children. The hazard of this kind of thing becomes apparent as we evaluate the teaching of the Scripture. Take time to evaluate 1 Thessalonians 2 and 1 Corinthians 1:18-2:16. Children are susceptible to "bandwagon" thinking. On one occasion a speaker succeeded in getting several children to say to a group, "Let's all go up and get saved." Spiritual wisdom causes one to question this kind of motivation.

On the other hand, the atmosphere may involve unnecessary distractions or discomforts that could have a negative influence. A speaker may stand with a bright light at his back, and children find it difficult to look at him. Sometimes the temperature may be too cold and damp. Or we may expect children to sit still too long. Remember that for a child to sit still is tiring and to move is relaxing, while for an adult the opposite is true.

Perhaps one of the greatest distractions is the distraction caused by other people. On one occasion a camp counselor was sitting in a small classroom talking with a child who seemed to be interested in salvation. Right in the middle of a serious conversation the child's interest seemed to vanish, and she became fidgety and eager to leave. It was only later that the counselor realized that several friends of the child had begun looking through the window and making faces. This social distraction seemed to spoil it all. Fortunately, the child's desire was genuine, and several hours later she came back ready to trust Christ. This incident illustrates the necessity of preventing a negative atmosphere.

One final appeal relating to atmosphere has to do with the use of music. Music has always been a part of the life of the people of God. The ministry of sacred music in church history is distinct, one that ought to be fully cultivated. However, we are all aware of the emotions that can be awakened as a result of music. Many people admit that hearing the opening strains of the hymn "Just As I Am" nearly brings tears to their eyes. The Christian who gives the Spirit the full and complete opportunity to accomplish the work of conviction will be careful in coupling music with appeals in evangelism.

3

Guidelines for Child Evangelism

It seems appropriate to begin with an overview of methods and techniques expressed in two different ways. First, we must avoid any tendency to oversimplify the process of child evangelism. Personalities are complex, and there is a vast array of individual differences to be considered.

At this point it may be helpful to focus attention on the doctrine/method issue. For those who are committed to the authority of Scripture and the supernatural nature of the Bible, doctrine cannot and must not change. We must be prepared even to lay down our lives for "the faith which was once for all delivered to the saints" (Jude 3). However, *method* not only may change but in many instances must change. There are many ways to demonstrate this fact, but perhaps the best is to look at the teaching ministry of Jesus. He was a master at a variety of methods, and He varied His methods with the situation and needs of the individuals to whom He ministered.

The virtue of wise, biblical living is to remain firm in doctrine and flexible in one's method of instruction. One of the great pitfalls for those who are conservatively minded is the tendency to revere method and hold to it as tenaciously as we hold to our doctrine. It appears that the only sure way to avoid this pitfall is to continue as a student of Bible doctrine. Thus we will have a basis for that discernment that distinguishes between doctrine and methodology.

In evangelism, although the gospel can be spelled out in doctrinal terms, and we must be prepared to use and explain those terms faithfully, a variety of approaches will be useful in communicating the gospel as we are sensitive to the leading of God. May He give us grace to avoid both compromising the message and oversimplifying the method.

One way to oversimplify methodology is to reduce evangelism to a given series of scriptural proof texts and imply that if we mechanically lead a person through these, the result will be salvation. Some may remember the "Roman road to salvation." This method involved a series of Scriptures from the book of Romans that was designed to be a step-by-step, surefire way to lead people to Christ. Some have found that in dealing with adults there are definite advantages in such approaches as the "Four Spiritual Laws" or other simplified methodology. As contradictory as it may seem, however, dealing with children requires more than a single step-by-step methodology.

The lack of mature understanding and thought patterns along with the naïveté and limited attention span of children makes the work of the evangelist one of unusual discernment and flexibility. We must strive to be flexible in ascertaining levels of need and understanding and to tailor the methodolody and approach to the needs of the child. Any prefabricated, step-by-step process will fall short.

In contrast, the second consideration of methods and techniques has to do with the glorious ease of the task! If a believer is a diligent and thorough student of the Scriptures and at the same time has a love and concern for children, leading children to Christ is not hard work. It is privileged, glorious business!

Personal evangelism is a matter of one-on-one Bible teaching. The basic task is to present the message of salvation in a way that is clearly understood and allows the Spirit freedom to do His perfect work of conviction. Although all of the dynamics of teaching are involved in this process, it is not difficult to adequately convey the gospel to children. We are not in this business alone, for we can be sure that the enablement of the Holy Spirit is a provision that God delights to make for His servants. One of my motives in preparing this study is to encourage those who are afraid to attempt leading a child to Christ. May you eagerly apply yourself to this glorious business, being confident of the presence and blessing of God. For the believer who knows the Scripture and walks with God, the task of child evangelism—while not a simple task —is gloriously easy.

Let us approach the discussion of techniques and methods by examining a series of don'ts and dos. There is no necessary order or sequence of importance in these. Rather it is hoped that the total impact will clarify and describe the easy but not simple task before us.

DON'TS

A strong consensus among spiritually minded teachers necessitates we face some warnings. Though our ministry must be life affirming and not life negating, there are some pitfalls to avoid. These include the following.

Don't "play God." We can pressure, force, or coerce a response from children and presumptuously move into an area that is the sole prerogative of the Holy Spirit. We may also play God by jumping too quickly to conclusions and evaluating opinions about children and their situation without properly listening or discerning.

Don't get locked into a prefabricated approach. Children's needs will be as varied as their faces, and we must always be concerned about the individuals—where they are in gaining knowledge of the truth as well as their readiness to respond to the convicting work of the Spirit. Children will have misunderstandings and misconceptions, and it may take a great deal of patience and some skill to discern their problems and minister to them. As I noted in chapter 1, the wise evangelist will keep in mind the necessary information that must be conveyed in an adequate presentation of the gospel.

Don't merely ask leading questions. Leading questions are questions that imply a desired answer and usually require only a "yes or no" response. Illustrations of leading questions include: "You all know that you are sinners going to hell, don't you? You know that Christ died for your sins, don't you? You know that by trusting Christ you will be saved from hell and on your way to heaven, don't you? You want to let Jesus come into your heart right now, don't you?" If an adult cannot lead a child or group of children to a series of "yes" responses with his personal influence and tone of voice then he is not very skilled at working with children. But one's leading children into a series of "yes" responses does not mean that they have been saved. Leading questions characterize quick and shoddy work in evangelism.

Don't confuse the child with too many illustrations, Scripture verses, or concepts. The attention span of a child and his or her simple pattern of thinking can be complicated by a profusion of ideas or Scripture. If you throw terms like *believe, trust, faith,* and *receive* at a child in one statement, you may generate perplexity. To jump from Revelation to Genesis and back again in a series of quotations may work against the child's understanding.

Don't expect "standard" terminology. Believers are familiar with and love certain expressions and terms. However, children may surprise us by sincerely using unconventional terminology. I remember one young person who, upon hearing the gospel for the first time, responded, "Wow, dis Jesus Christ stuff!" This was repeated three times before I could recover from my shock about such non-traditional language! Actually there was a deep and genuine response in this individual that became apparent in his growing interest in the gospel and eventual confession of Christ as Savior. Even in describing what has happened in their lives, many new believers will use non-traditional language. We need to be prepared to deal with them not only in traditional ways.

Don't always get the child unsaved first. This awkward statement is designed to counter the thinking that when a child expresses an interest in Christ it is assumed that the child is unsaved. Or we may assume that we must always make the child aware of his or her guilt and lost condition. Experienced adults find that a significant percentage of children who respond to a personal invitation are already believers. They may need help in assurance of salvation or dealing with sin in their lives. As noted previously, we can become part of the problem rather than a part of the solution if we unwittingly "recycle a profession" rather than intelligently ascertain where the child is spiritually.

Don't overemphasize fear. Fear or any other strong emotion wrongly used can cause us to run ahead of the Holy Spirit and precipitate a false profession. A certain amount of emotion is normal and healthy in response to the gospel, but we can overdo playing upon emotion to the detriment of the child.

Don't create false issues. False issues include matters such as raising the hand, kneeling, coming forward, talking to an adult, and any number of things that might be imposed upon a child arbitrarily. We know that none of these are necessary for salvation, but we can unwittingly make these issues important in the mind of a child and either frustrate or precipitate some type of shallow response. We must never forget that salvation is of the Lord.

Don't fail to give the opportunity to settle the issue of salvation now. Skillful salesmen point out that one weaknesses in many evangelistic efforts is that we fail to "close the deal." Since we are reluctant to force a profession, we may err on the other side and not make the urgency of the response clear. The message of the gospel *is* an urgent one, and we must not leave the issue of the child's personal response indefinite.

Don't insist the child get saved now. This is the other side of the coin. We may insist to the point that we do not let the work of the Holy Spirit come to maturity. Many testify to having been pushed into a false profession by over-eager evangelists.

Don't fabricate a prayer. At this point some readers may take issue with me. It seems common among evangelicals to lead children to "pray the sinners prayer." I am personally convinced that if the work of the Holy Spirit has come to maturity and the child has been adequately and carefully instructed, there is no need to fabricate a prayer. We may need to tell the child that he or she needs to speak to the Lord Jesus to tell Him of his or her need and desire for salvation. But it seems quite apparent that if one cannot express to the Savior the natural desire for Him and His salvation, we must doubt if the work of the Holy Spirit is complete. God does not shut off the thinking processes of the child in the crucial issue of conviction and salvation. Rather, He would say now as He did long ago, "Come now, and let us reason together" (Isaiah 1:18).

Don't tell the child he or she is saved—let the Word of God do that. Those who have been with a child who is genuinely exercised about salvation and have heard those beautiful childlike cries to the Lord for salvation know what a great temptation it is to say, "Wonderful, now you are saved!" Even if the child prays in your presence and intelligently and sincerely invites Jesus Christ to be his or her Savior, please don't lay the foundation of assurance of salvation in your words. Rather, turn the attention of the child right back to the passage of Scripture that you were using to point him to Christ, and let that speak to him and give him the first foundation for his assurance of salvation. You may have heard the expression "The blood secures; the Word assures." We may

encourage and instruct as we lay the foundation for assurance. But let
the Word of God tell the child he is saved.

Don't think your job is over when a profession is made. In one sense,
follow-up work is outside the scope of this discussion. But to do evangelistic work without efforts of follow-up borders on the unethical. Though
all individuals who come to Christ need follow-up ministries, it is a particularly urgent matter with children. We should carefully and prayerfully develop ways to follow up and support those efforts with
intercessory prayer as the apostle Paul and others did.

DOS

At this point let us turn to the positive ingredients of leading children to Christ. You will note my attempt to avoid a mechanical prefabricated method. Prayerfully consider the following:

Do be available and accessible. Some adults have worked with children for years and have never had the privilege of dealing face-to-face
with a child who has expressed an interest in becoming saved. Sunday
school teachers who rush into class late, then gather up their books and
dash away as soon as the closing bell rings, will rarely have such a privilege. Camp counselors who spend virtually all their time either hobnob-
bing with fellow counselors or fighting with energetic campers will
rarely have such a privilege. In fact, one of the advantages in using visual aids in teaching children is that it gives a few minutes to naturally
hang around after class to pick up the pieces and gather up the materials. This is available and accessible time for children to approach. We
need to consciously cultivate our skills of availability.

It is a rare and desperate child who will approach adults who are
rushing preoccupied through life. For the most part, it will take a good
bit of courage for a child to approach an adult to ask for further discussion or help with their spiritual concerns. Genuine love and accep-
tance, relaxed and friendly contacts, and patience and physical
accessibility will result in opportunities to minister to children. Many of
us need to discipline ourselves to take time to display the attitudes of
availability.

Do facilitate the conviction of the Spirit. In John 16:7-11 the unique
work of the Holy Spirit is described. He will convict the unsaved of sin,
righteousness, and judgment. Fortunately, the Lord Jesus described

these three dimensions of conviction to us.

First, the Lord Jesus described the conviction of sin. Note Jesus did not say "sins." The Spirit has always convicted people of sins. The unique work of the Spirit now is to convict individuals specifically of the sin of unbelief, the ultimately condemning sin. As the Lord told Nicodemus, "He who does not believe has been judged already, because he has not believed in the name of the only begotten Son of God" (John 3:18). In the light of the finished work of Christ, the cardinal sin is the sin of unbelief. We must make sure that our ministry of the gospel emphasizes the issue of unbelief and the command of the gospel that requires the obedience of faith in Christ.

Second, the Lord Jesus described the conviction of righteousness. Jesus did not say *un*righteousness. Again we must note that the work of the Holy Spirit through all history has been that of convicting men and women of unrighteousness. Our Lord taught His disciples—and us—that the unique work of the Spirit in this age is to convict the world of righteousness: "Concerning righteousness, because I go to the Father, and you no longer behold Me" (John 16:10). Only the righteousness of God qualifies one for the presence of God. The Lord Jesus inherently possessed that righteousness and thus was qualified to be received back to the throne in heaven. The Holy Spirit makes people aware that without the righteousness of Christ they will never follow Christ to heaven.

Scripture describes two kinds of righteousness. The first is a righteousness derived from obedience to the law (Philippians 3:9). Human righteousness, however experienced and developed, will never qualify us for heaven. The gospel message is a message that reveals God's righteousness (Romans 3:21-28) as a different *kind* of righteousness. This kind or quality of righteousness alone qualifies one for heaven. It is not generated by human effort but is received by faith when one receives Christ as Savior. In salvation Christ is made unto us righteousness (1 Corinthians 1:30). This righteousness is offered to all in the Person of Christ but is upon all those who believe (Romans 3:22). The conviction of the Holy Spirit convinces people that without the righteousness of Christ they will never follow the Savior to heaven. We need to make sure that our presentation of the gospel gives the Spirit the equipment to work with in bringing that conviction.

Third, the Lord Jesus described the conviction of judgment. Although many properly fear a judgment to come, the Lord Jesus taught that the unique work of conviction by the Spirit emphasized a judgment already passed: "The ruler of this world has been judged" (John 16:11). The judgment of Satan and his host became a reality in the death and resurrection of Christ (Colossians 2:14-15). The idea that good and evil are struggling in the world and we are eagerly waiting to see which side wins is a false notion derived from pagan philosophy and religion. We already know who is Victor! Christ has triumphed over the host of evil, and He is already the victorious One. We merely wait for the fulfillment and manifestation of that victory. Satan is already a condemned foe, and his cause is already lost.

It is futile to hold out against the claims of Christ, for the issue is already settled. Nothing is to be gained, but everything is to be lost in remaining in unbelief.

The gospel should be presented to children as well as all others in light of the necessary work of the Spirit in conviction. As spokesmen for God, we should desire that our efforts will enhance the work of the Spirit and in no way replace or preempt that necessary work. We have the glorious confidence that God will faithfully do His work, for He "desires all men to be saved and to come to the knowledge of the truth" (1 Timothy 2:4).

Do draw out the child. We can develop skill in finding out what a child understands or misunderstands in regard to the gospel and ascertain his readiness to receive Christ. Rather than a series of leading questions, ask the child to explain the way of salvation. Pose a situation in which a friend asks how one can know how to get to heaven. Listen to the child's answer discerningly, for in such a response you will be able to detect what the child does or does not understand about salvation.

Do correct incorrect or inadequate understanding. If you take time to listen to a child and draw him out, you will probably be amazed at the inadequate or incorrect elements of his concept of biblical truth. Remember, an important way to look at personal evangelism is to see it as a specialized form of one-on-one teaching. We can systematically explore areas of truth and understanding that are a part of the message. Of course, this requires us to be thoroughly grounded in the doctrines of salvation. And it should be noted that I am not implying that the child must become a theologian before he or she can trust Christ. But it is important to view personal evangelism as refined and specialized teaching of biblical truth.

Do stress the urgency of salvation. This can be done without manipulation. We need to make children aware of the urgency of salvation. In fact, it is to believers that the apostle Paul says, "Now is the day of salvation" (2 Corinthians 6:2, KJV). The specific personal response of faith in Christ is God's one condition for salvation. We must make this crystal clear to children and remind them that we do not have the promise of tomorrow.

Do stick to the basic issues. At this point I will briefly refer to the discussion of necessities in chapter 1 to refresh our minds on the basic issues involved in presenting the gospel. We must learn the lesson that is so vividly conveyed by the Lord Jesus in His conversation with the woman of Samaria in John 4. He appropriately responded to her questions that potentially sidetracked His train of thought. But He was careful to press the essential issue of her personal need and His ability to provide for all of her needs in His saving grace. Though adults may sometimes intentionally sidetrack an evangelist to avoid pressure, children may also unwittingly divert an adult with all sorts of questions and issues that pop into their minds. It is our responsibility to be disciplined to keep the conversation on track.

Do use the Bible. If at all possible, open the Bible, look at it, read from it, have the child read a portion, and in other obvious ways convey the fact that the message we present comes from the written Word of God. People can be saved through the spoken word, and God is pleased to bless the spoken word of testimony (Romans 10:17). But it is important for children to associate the message with written Scripture. Remember, the Bible will be around and available to them long after you or I have left. The fact that we use the Bible and establish this pattern in their minds may be important in their own attitudes towards Scripture and their faithfulness in reading and studying it. In the final analysis, we teach as much or more by example as we do by precept.

After all, it is His Word that God has promised to bless (Isaiah 55:10-11), not necessarily our illustrations, cleverness, or cute expressions.

Do teach the need, concept, and urgency of faith. At this point I must emphasize the necessity of understanding the key terms *faith* and *believe*. Few Christians have actually made an adequate study of these essential terms. In the New Testament these two words have the same root: one is a verb, one is a noun. In essence they have the same meaning and refer to that firm and welcome conviction about Christ, His person, and His Work that results in obedient response. We must help children understand the difference between mere mental assent to facts and true biblical faith and belief. This is one of the areas where the evangelist must be a diligent student of Bible doctrine. If you can't explain to a child in accurate, valid biblical terms the meaning of *faith* or *believe*, you will find yourself very limited in effectiveness.

Do encourage the child to communicate with the Lord Jesus. Saving faith has its object in the Person of Christ. He is a living Savior and knows the inaudible thoughts and cries of our hearts. The child needs to understand that salvation comes through Christ, not the evangelist. If a child wants to be saved he or she must deal with the Savior. We must get out of the way and make sure that Christ is the focal point of our message and our method. If Christ is properly presented in communicating the gospel, it will be natural for the child to commune with Him.

Although salvation is not through prayer but through faith in Christ, it is biblically clear that that faith involves receiving Christ and establishing a personal relationship with Him. It may be important in cases where the child has not prayed audibly to ask the child to tell you if he or she talked with the Lord Jesus. Ask the child to tell you what he or she said to Him. Since Scripture teaches that "everyone who calls on the name of the Lord shall be saved" (Acts 2:21), our goal as evangelists is to see children come to the point in which they call upon the Lord Jesus.

Do inquire about and review what the child did and said in receiving Christ. This is not a matter of unduly prying into a child's private life but rather expressing interest in the child and making sure the expression of faith was biblical. At this point some misunderstandings may need to be cleared up through careful, patient Bible teaching.

Do follow up. The Great Commission given by the Lord Jesus to His disciples (Matthew 28:18-20) makes clear that our responsibility is not only that of evangelism or the making of disciples but also baptizing and teaching.

One of the most significant things for an evangelist to recognize is that his presence with the child who has just trusted Christ is in the most crucial "moment of readiness" for the first aspects of follow-up. It is urgent that we immediately get the child back into an examination of the Scripture passage that we used in pointing him to Christ. Let that Scripture become the foundation for his assurance of salvation. Let us use these moments strategically and wisely and set a pattern of looking into God's Word for instruction and encouragement.

Proper follow-up always involves an emphasis upon the child's reading and studying the Word of God. There is no substitute for this in the Christian life. This may be accomplished and enhanced in a number of ways. First, there are booklets for children who have just trusted Christ. These encourage and illustrate simple ways of Bible study and review the essential ingredients of a growing Christian life. In addition to the study of the Word of God, children also need to learn the importance of a regular and disciplined prayer life, witnessing to others about their faith, dealing with sin in a biblical way, choosing proper Christian friends, and seeking fellowship in a local church where the Word of God is taught.

Another specific suggestion for follow-up is the use of correspondence courses. Such materials as the children's correspondence courses produced by Emmaus Bible College are highly recommended. This is a particularly effective alternative if the adult will not have personal access to the child.

Your own personal contact will be one of the most effective ways to accomplish this important task. Children are keenly impressed by efforts of adults to visit them and take time to talk with them. This gives the adult an opportunity to talk with the child and assess his problems as well as his progress and make a more specific attempt to meet his needs.

Sometimes the one who leads the child to Christ does not have exposure to him on a long-term basis. In such cases it is often possible to get the child's address and make contact with a mature and knowledgeable Christian who lives in the same area. Ask that person to step in and provide some follow-up ministry. It is important to let the child know either through a conversation, a phone call, or a letter that you have asked an adult to do that. This will help pave the way for a more receptive response from both the child and his family. It may take some questioning and searching to find such an adult, but asking a fellow believer to follow-up has good biblical precedent (Philippians 2:19-23).

In light of the unique needs of children, it is particularly important to be concerned about their choice of friends. First Corinthians 15:33-34 stresses our responsibility to make the right choice of those with whom we closely associate. One effective follow-up is to encourage the child to establish the right kind of personal friendships as well as church fellowship. In fact, if a child moves into teenage years without establishing good Christian friendships and loyalty to a local church, it is unlikely that he will make it through adolescence without some serious or tragic spiritual default.

The development of a believer's prayer life and his witness for Christ are also vital aspects of biblical living that should be considered in follow-up. Each of these areas could be the subject for an entire study, and there is no thought of minimizing the importance of prayer, witness, and service for Christ in this brief reference. These will not necessarily and automatically become a part of the life of a child who trusts Christ. Children must be cultivated and taught, and it becomes our responsibility to be diligent in fulfilling all aspects of our responsibility.

4

How-To Illustrations

Let us in this chapter consider four children, having differing problems, and the conversations that the Lord used to bring their conviction/salvation experience to fruition.

CHUCK: A LACK OF UNDERSTANDING

Darkness settled over the little valley. I was both counselor of older boys and bugler for the week of Bible camp. Out of sheer necessity I kept the bugle locked in my car. I had just finished blowing "taps" that night and was locking the car when a hand reached out of the darkness and firmly grasped my arm. I was startled when I saw my problem camper, Chuck. My surprise increased when he said in careful, calculated words, "Mr. Dan, I need to get saved tonight."

To say that Chuck was a problem camper is an understatement. A Christian man who lived in Chuck's neighborhood had bailed him out of jail on the condition that he would come to camp. Chuck claimed that he did not know it would be a Bible camp, and the first evening at devotion time he was highly indignant, implying that he had been trapped into coming. For a sixteen-year-old young man, he not only had experienced a lot in life, but he had developed a certain charisma in leadership. He was always going in the opposite direction from which everyone else in the camp intended to go. That was particularly true when it was time for chapel or devotions. He was hostile to anything of a spiritual nature and demonstrated a pained look through the entire study. I was convinced that nothing that was said at camp was making any impact on Chuck. So I was thoroughly surprised when he said he needed to be saved.

We made our way into an empty cabin. I started with several logical questions: "Why do you say you want to get saved? Why do you want to get saved *tonight?*" It was apparent that he was experiencing deep conviction of sin. He said, "I knew I was bad before I came to camp, but I know that what I call bad was really sin. I'm a sinner for sure."

There was such urgency in Chuck's voice that I could scarcely believe this was the same person who had been indifferent during the camp sessions. A further question revealed Chuck's limited use of biblical terminology. I asked him what he meant when he said he wanted to get saved. He struggled for words, trying in a number of ways to simply say that he knew that he was in trouble with a holy God, sensing this much in the same way that he had understood being in trouble with the law. His brief and unpleasant encounter with the penal system had made deep impressions upon him. And he said that he knew hell must be far worse than jail. He indicated that his understanding of being saved meant that in some way things could be cleared or made right between himself and God. He wanted to be free from a miserable sense of guilt and the newfound fear of some day facing a holy God.

Chuck's obvious lack of biblical teaching led me to quickly summarize the biblical perspective of man's need and God's provision. I went back to the creation, the Fall of man, the tragic history of man in his sin, the coming of Jesus Christ into the world, His sinless life, and His substitutionary sacrificial death. When I went on to talk about the resurrection of Christ, it was obvious that I had left Chuck behind. With a puzzled look he said, "Run that by me again." I went back to the creation and the Fall of man and quickly moved again through the coming of Christ and His sacrificial death. The puzzled look was still on Chuck's face, and he repeated his request, "Run that by me again."

I repeated it once again. Since there was nothing wrong with Chuck's level of intellectual comprehension, his repeated request to review the plan of salvation puzzled me. I asked him if there was any part that he did not understand. He indicated that he could not understand how something Jesus did nearly two thousand years ago could help him.

He did not understand the biblical doctrines of substitution, redemption, and propitiation.

Rather than moving into a long doctrinal dissertation, I resorted to a standard object lesson. I held out my left hand, open and palm up. I said, "Chuck, let this hand represent you." I reached into my pocket, pulled out a small key case, laid it in my open palm, and said, "Let this key case represent your sin. God looks down from heaven, and what does He see?"

Chuck's answer was simple and immediate: "He sees me with my sin on me."

Then I held out my right hand, open with the palm up. I said, "Chuck, let this hand represent the Lord Jesus Christ. He had no sin on Him, no sin in Him; He was holy and perfect in all His ways. The Father speaking from heaven publicly acclaimed that He was fully satisfied with the perfection of His Son. But the Lord Jesus went to the cross of Calvary. Men nailed Him there because they hated Him and wanted to do away with Him. They did not realize that they were fulfilling the plan of God that required that a Savior die for us sinners. While the Lord Jesus was hanging on the cross, God, who knew your sins and mine even two thousand years ago, laid our sins on Him."

At that point I transferred the key case from my left hand to my right hand. Chuck watched intently, and I continued, "Now God looks down from heaven—and what does He see? He sees sin on the Substitute and judges Him to death for that sin."

I invited Chuck to strike my right hand. He not only knocked my hand down but knocked off the key case. I continued, "Christ died because of your sin. And in His death He put your sin away; He satisfied all of God's righteous claims and judgment against your sin and mine. In fact, the resurrection of Christ proves that this great task was accomplished. Christ rose the third day—sin had been dealt with and put away." I began to raise my right hand, now empty. "Then the Lord Jesus ascended back into heaven and was received at the right side of the Father. He had finished the great work of salvation in our behalf."

After giving Chuck a few seconds to contemplate, I called his attention to my now-empty left hand. "Now, Chuck, where are your sins?" His eyes filled with tears, and he jumped to his feet. "They're gone!" The thrill of seeing this young man comprehend the glorious meaning of Scripture "Christ died for our sins" was worth many times over the grief that he had caused me during the early part of the week.

It seemed fitting at that point to invite Chuck to settle the matter of his salvation by receiving and acknowledging Jesus Christ to be his Savior and sin bearer. The delight that registered on his face indicated that that glorious and simple transaction of faith was possibly already a fact. But I urged him to speak to the Lord Jesus, acknowledging his need as a sinner and his gratitude to the Lord Jesus for dying for his sin.

I was grateful that Chuck felt free to pray out loud. One would never have suspected that this was his first prayer, for he spoke naturally and fluently as he told the Lord the story of his life of sin, admitted his deep need, and recounted what he had just come to understand about the Lord Jesus' dying for his sins. He thanked Christ for taking away his sin and told Him he wanted Him to be his Savior.

When Chuck finished his prayer we sat in silence for a few moments. I repeated a question that I had asked earlier: "Chuck, where are your sins?" His answer was joyous and simple: "Jesus took them away!"

Jim: A Lack of Mature Conviction

I met Jim the week I was counseling at another Bible camp. I was assigned the youngest group of campers, most of whom were only eight years of age. Two of my campers were twin brothers. They were not only small, but they were only seven years old. Still, their energy and alertness made up for whatever they lacked in size, and it became apparent at the beginning of the week that they were going to set the pace for the rest of the cabin.

One of that particular camp's standards was that each camper learn two memory verses during the rest period after lunch. One of the twins, Jim, skillfully rattled off his verses each day. On Friday he came into my room to say his verses, but he was obviously ill prepared. He stumbled through, glancing at his open Bible. The matter-of-fact way in which he faked his way through his memory work prompted my comment: "Jim, you're not too interested in this Bible memory work, are you?" His response startled me. "Mr. Dan, I'm sick and tired of all this memory business. I memorize verses for Sunday school, I memorize verses for Awana clubs, and I memorized more verses than you can count to earn my way to camp. I'm tired of memorizing."

Since I had not yet had a chance for an extended personal contact with him, I tried to continue the conversation. "With all that memory of Scripture, you certainly must clearly understand the way of salvation, right?"

"Oh, yes, I know that to be saved you must believe in the Lord Jesus Christ for your personal salvation." At that point he added a number of other statements that were so fluently and skillfully expressed, I thought he was fast on his way to becoming a great preacher.

I was impressed with his response, and in a somewhat reflective way I said to him, "Obviously you have been saved for a few years."

To my great surprise he snapped back, "Nope, I'm not saved." I was so shocked that I did not know how to respond. In fact, I could not believe that this biblically articulate young boy would have the audacity to come up with that kind of answer. But having given me his answer, he volunteered nothing further.

When I recovered from shock my inclination was to really go after him. I wanted to threaten him and shake his young soul over the flames of hell!

Several moments of awkward silence were suddenly interrupted by the camp bell, signaling the end of the rest period. He immediately began to fidget and became eager to be on his way. It was apparent that for all of his knowledge of the Scriptures and his detailed understanding of the way of salvation, the conviction of the Spirit had not yet come to maturity. I also realized that he was skillful enough to make a profession just to get me off his case. So I simply said to him, "Jim, I hope you realize you're playing a dangerous spiritual game. To know the way of salvation and yet boldly reject Christ is a serious thing." With that I sent him on his way.

Repeatedly I thought of the bold way in which he declared that he was not saved. I wondered how an individual could be "gospel hardened" at the tender age of seven. Even as I tried to pray for him, I scarcely knew how to express my perplexity at his condition. Yet it was apparent that his great need was to experience the true and mature work of the conviction of the Spirit.

That night was the planned camp fire and testimony time for the week of camp. I had to lead singing, so my junior counselor corralled the boys near the fire. By the time we had finished singing, the camp director had several fellows in line ready to give their testimonies. I had not noticed him previously, but the first camper who stepped forward to give his testimony was Jim! He launched into his testimony at full speed, speaking as fluently as an experienced evangelist: "I am so thankful that I have received the Lord Jesus Christ as my personal Savior. It's a wonderful thing to know that my sins are forgiven and that I am no longer bound for a lost eternity. I thank the Lord for saving me and giving me the assurance that I am on my way to heaven." He sat down.

I was again in a state of shock. Then I found myself grinding my teeth and saying under my breath, "You little hypocrite, wait till I get my hands on you!" Needless to say, I didn't hear the other testimonies. My mind was racing with questions. How could a boy this young perpetrate such skillful deception?

As soon as the camp fire was over, I grabbed Jim, looked him straight in the face, and said, "Young man, you and I have some talking to do. You told me at noon today that you were not saved, and tonight you stand here at the camp fire and give us this line. Who do you think you're trying to deceive?"

He struggled to speak but managed to say in a pleading voice, "But Mr. Dan, I *did* get saved."

Obviously we needed to talk. We went back into my room. As he spoke to me the almost haughty and indifferent tone of voice that I heard at noon was replaced by a sincere attempt to communicate.

"My team had a volleyball game this afternoon," he said, "and I was kind of anxious to get out and play after rest period. While we were playing the game I thought about what you said about playing a dangerous game with God. In fact, I was thinking about it so much that I really missed a couple of easy shots and had my team angry with me.

"I left the game and went back up to my cabin to look for you. I went into your room, but you weren't there. So I sat on your bed and began to think. I thought of some young people who had died who were about my age. I thought of being lost forever. I wanted to run and find you and talk to you. But then I realized I didn't need you to get saved.

"I got on my knees right by your bed and prayed to the Lord Jesus. I told Him how ashamed I was that I had known that I was a sinner and how to be saved for a long time and that I was ashamed that I had not trusted Him. I asked Him to come into my life and save me from my sins. And I remembered that the Bible said, 'Whosoever shall call upon the Lord shall be saved,' and I knew that I was saved."

We sat in silence for a few moments, and then he continued in a pleading voice, "So you see, Mr. Dan, I did get saved, and I am thankful to the Lord it's all settled."

In the next few minutes we shared some tears. I was silently thanking the Lord that He had not only brought the work of conviction to maturity, but that He had kept me from my human impulse to pressure him earlier that afternoon. Salvation is of the Lord—every aspect of it!

MARY: TOO MUCH RELIGION

I had just completed the third lesson in a series of vacation Bible school sessions. I was teaching the gospel, using an illustrative chart that I had adapted for children from the old "Two Roads and Two Destinies" chart used by evangelists a generation ago. We had covered the biblical truths concerning the creation and Fall of man, the broad road that leads to destruction, the reality of physical death, and the certain fact of future judgment for those who die without Christ.

After class, I fiddled with my drawing pens and was getting ready to put the partially completed chart in a secure place when I noticed that one of the girls was standing nearby in awkward silence. After a brief greeting, I asked Mary if she was enjoying vacation Bible school. She said this was the first VBS that she had attended but that she had been here each of the first three nights. There was again an awkward silence. It was apparent that she wanted to talk with me, but conversation was not coming easy.

To draw her out I asked if she understood the Scripture lessons. Immediately it was apparent that was precisely what she wanted to talk about. "I think so," Mary said, "but at my church we never talk about death or being lost forever." She described one occasion in which her grandmother had read a book to her that talked about people being lost in hell. Her mother had interrupted and expressed her displeasure with the grandmother. Mary had admitted that she had thought about the matter off and on for a period of several years. Now, as an eleven-year-old, she was hearing the message again.

I asked if she knew what God had done to provide salvation for her so that she would not have to go to a lost eternity.

"Well, I'm sure that I have to go to church and be good." After a pause she added, "I do go to church, and I try to be good."

I was impressed by the fact that in her troubled condition she mentioned nothing about Christ, the Bible, or any other aspect of the biblical teaching concerning salvation. She knew nothing but a system of good works, and it was obviously not satisfying to her.

I took out a smaller completed version of the chart that I was using. The completed chart included the cross of Calvary and the open door to salvation—the narrow way that leads to eternal life. Mary listened intently as I spoke of the Lord Jesus and His sacrificial death.

She mentioned that on two occasions she had heard about some miracles that Jesus performed and specifically remembered that He had accepted a little boy's lunch. But the thought of Christ's death or the matter of His being a sin bearer was totally new to her. I invited her to read several passages of Scripture relating to the finished work of Christ and urged her to come for the remaining lessons. She assured me that she would come back.

In the succeeding lessons I noticed Mary sat near the front and followed every word. I prayed that she would understand the plan of salvation and that the Spirit would be able to triumph over the system of works with which she had been indoctrinated.

After the class on Friday, I found Mary standing quietly at my side. "Hello, Mary," I said. "I'm glad you've continued to come to our vacation Bible school sessions."

Mary's response was pointed. She said earnestly, "I want to go to heaven where Jesus is, and I'm not sure how."

I picked up her last statement. "What do you mean you're not sure?"

"I think about dying and being lost forever. I know God loves me, but I've sinned against Him."

"Yes, God loves you, Mary. And because He loves you He did something to provide salvation for you. Do you understand that?"

"I understand that Jesus died for my sins. But how can I know that I'm going to heaven?"

I invited her to open her Bible to the first chapter of John. I urged her to read verse 12. We discussed *believing* in the Lord Jesus and *receiv-*

ing Him. We talked about receiving a person and specifically about inviting, or extending a welcome, to a person. I asked her to read the verse again. When she finished she looked up and said, "I want to do this, right now."

She bowed her head, and we sat in silence for several moments. There was no outward evidence of what was going on. Then she opened her eyes and looked up at me.

I asked, "Well, what did you do?"

"I prayed," she said. "I talked to Jesus."

"What did you say to Him?"

"I told Him I could never be good enough to go to heaven because I was a sinner. I told Him I was glad I had learned that He died for my sins—and that now I wanted Him to be my Savior."

"Do you think He heard you?" I asked.

She seemed puzzled for a moment, and then her face brightened. "Yes, He knows what I think and what I say in my heart."

"What about going to heaven?" I asked.

This repeated question seemed to puzzle her all over again. We turned our attention back to John 1:12 and focused on the result of believing and receiving Christ: "To them He gave the right to become children of God."

"To whom did He give that right?" I asked.

"To them," she answered.

I pushed her Bible a little closer and asked, "Who is *them?*"

She looked intently at the verse. In a minute she looked up, smiled, and said, "The people that receive Jesus."

I waited for several moments, which seemed like an eternity. She was deep in thought, and I obviously did not need to stimulate her thoughts with questions.

Then came that delightful positive response, "And I am one of those people—I have received Christ."

"So what does it mean that God has given you when you received Christ?"

Her response came as her eyes focused upon the verse again. "The right to be called a child of God. I am His child!"

OUR DAUGHTER: GENUINE FAITH

Adults tend to doubt a child's confession of faith in Christ. Let me, with some embarrassment, illustrate this from my own family.

I was teaching a special series of children's classes at a local church in the city where we lived. As a visual basis for these lessons, I was using the "Two Roads" chart referred to earlier. This chart is designed to assist in understanding Jesus' teaching concerning the broad road that leads to destruction and the narrow road that leads to life (Matthew 7:13-14).

On Thursday night we concluded the meeting, gathered up all the paraphernalia that is a necessary part of such activities, and returned to our car. As I prepared to start the car, my four-year-old daughter, standing behind me, put her hand on my shoulder. "Daddy," she said, "don't start the car until I tell you and Mom something very important." There was a pause, and then she continued, "I got saved tonight."

At that point one part of me wanted literally to jump through the roof shouting, "Hallelujah!" This was my oldest daughter and the first of my children to express any direct interest in spiritual things. However, a second surge of emotion followed. *Don't be too hasty,* I thought. *She is very young. She probably doesn't know what she's talking about.*

She was only four. But she had already started kindergarten, and all seemed to be going well with her schooling. She had been exposed to Bible teaching from her earliest days, and even though we could not recall significant conversation about her personal salvation prior to this, we had certainly been praying for this moment even from before her birth.

She continued, "That man said that if we knew we were sinners and on the broad road that leads to destruction, we should speak to the Lord Jesus and acknowledge to Him that we were sinners, thank Him for dying on the cross for our sins, and invite Him to come into our lives and be our Savior from sin." "That man" was her father, but she was in such deep thought that that was what she recounted.

Both my wife and I interrogated her, and to our surprise she withstood the test. We inquired about other aspects of her understanding of the issues of sin and salvation and found her to be thinking clearly. She was convinced that she had actually spoken to the Lord Jesus. Since that is what the Bible required her to do, and since the Lord always saves those who call upon Him, she repeatedly confessed her salvation to be real.

Needless to say, it was a joyful trip home. She had responded so positively to our further questioning that I assumed the strong backwash of doubt that I had experienced earlier had been resolved. But to be honest, it still lurked in the recesses of my mind.

Later that night my wife and I talked about the incident, and I was surprised to find that she too had experienced the same mixed emotions. She was only four and small for her age. We certainly didn't want to see her move through life with a false profession, and yet we were overjoyed with the clear evidence of her response to the gospel. (I should mention that to this day as an adult our daughter maintains the same strong conviction that she received Christ as Savior that night.)

Our mixed emotions, however, had registered on her young mind. The next day when she came home from school she greeted my wife with these words: "Mom, you and Dad really don't believe me, do you?"

The statement caught my wife off guard, and she asked what she meant. "You and Dad really don't believe that I got saved last night." It was apparent that she had read our doubts, and this had been rather predominant in her thinking during the day. My wife sat down and talked with her at great length, admitting the measure of doubt and trying to explain it. But for some reason she did not feel that the issue was entirely settled in our daughter's mind. After that conversation our daughter went out and sat on the front steps of our house waiting for my return home.

My wife called me at the office and kindly warned me, "There is a little girl waiting for you on our front steps. She has an important question to ask you."

When I arrived home my daughter met me with the same question that she had asked of her mother, "You and Mom don't believe that I really got saved last night, do you?" At that point I had to face up to her awareness of my mixed response and how this would be worked out for her good. I had to admit that I had mixed emotions and tried to explain this on the basis of her youth. Her testimony was clear and insistent, however, and in the process of talking with her further both my wife and I came to the realization that we had followed the easy pattern of doubting a child's confession of faith just because she was a child. We are grateful that our sincere apologies for our unbelief were accepted. And we were not only delighted with those early responses of her confession of faith in Christ but also rejoiced in seeing a number of steps of progress in the faith that characterized her young life and, in fact, continue to bring us delight in her adult life.

Let me conclude this illustration by saying that we are grateful that we participated in a local church that was ready to genuinely accept a child's confession of faith and give children the opportunity to move on in the normal steps of Christian growth including such matters as believer's baptism and full fellowship in that church.

Each of the foregoing illustrations differs in many ways, and yet all reflect the process of being a careful and patient communicator of the gospel, earnestly trying to discern the level of spiritual understanding and conviction as the Spirit does His perfect work.

Epilogue

Let us consider one final word of encouragement. In a coming day when we will stand in the presence of the Lord, we will understand in a new way that all that God is going to salvage out of history is people. When the dust of time has settled and eternity is upon us, we may be impressed at what we will *not* find. God is not going to salvage our cars, houses, bank accounts, libraries, or even our computers and sophisticated gadgets for space travel. All that He is going to salvage is *people*. To borrow the thoughts of the apostle Peter, seeing that all these *things* are going to be incinerated, what kind of people should we be? What kind of investment should we make with our lives? Any of the energies invested in ministering to people will be directly in keeping with the purposes and plans of God. We may fritter away time in many pursuits, but there is no better investment of our lives than that of reaching people with the message of eternal life through the Lord Jesus.

When a child is won to Christ, not only is his soul saved, but a life is saved for the glory of the Savior. Winning children to Christ is a wonderful business with eternal implications. May we shun the careless and slipshod job that comes so easily. There are many forces and voices at work in our world clamoring for the attention, the minds, and the energies of children. May we give our best energies to reach the young for Christ, to serve the Master with the best of our energies, and to go about the Lord's business with a care and a diligence born of spiritual discernment and biblical commitment that will earn His commendation, "Well done, thou good and faithful servant" (Matthew 25:21).

Think back to your last bad haircut. If your barber or stylist didn't follow the contours of your head, a part of your hair might have stuck up or out. Your haircut looked bad.